No Debt Zone

Your 9 Step Guide
to a Debt Free Life

ASHLEY BREWSTER

ISBN: 9781086456462

CONTENTS

ACKNOWLEDGMENTS

I want to thank everyone who ever made an impact on my life. I want to especially thank my parents, Alfred and Renee Brewster, for always providing me with a life that encouraged and inspired me to do better. I want to also thank my godmother, Carol Wade, for her years of financial education to make me believe that wealth was possible for me.

I also want to thank you for reading! I hope you learn something that completely changes   your   financial   future!

INTRODUCTION

Is all debt bad debt? This question is often misleading. The question you should be asking yourself is, "how many years of my life will I spend paying it back?" If the answer is longer than two years, you truly cannot afford the purchase. The world makes you believe that "good debt" is what you use to acquire assets. But the only winners are the lenders. We have been misled into financial prisons disguised as mortgages, car notes, and student loans. These are all debts that are considered "good" by societal standards with the idea that these types of debt provide tax benefits or advantages in life. But at what cost? When you cannot make the

1

payments, whether you have good debt or bad debt, the outcome is the same; financial ruin.

A job is supposed to be a means to an end. A job was never supposed to be an end to your dreams or what you did until you die due to debt.

We often get too comfortable in what others think we should have according to the false realities that are showcased on social media. Once we stop caring about the opinions of others, not only will our self-esteem increase but so will our net worth.

The purpose of this book is to help you create your own, personal no debt zone. I will teach you how to manage your debt, and then eliminate your debt. The less debt you have, the more likely you are to become financially free. The more financially free you are, the better off your life will be. Ask yourself, if I did not have debt, would my job and the stress it brings be necessary?

I have a plan for you. A plan that will change your life. In this 9 Step Plan, I will teach you how to become completely debt free for the rest of your life. This process will only take up to 60 months to complete. Within 24 months, you will be consumer debt free. I will explain consumer debt in depth later. It is time to buy back your freedom, but your freedom is 100 percent dependent upon you.

STEP 1:

ASSESS WHERE YOU ARE

You may think that because I am a millennial that I have never struggled with money or that I have always been financially savvy. That is not the case at all. As a college graduate, I racked up close to $20,000 of debt that I carried right into my early stages of adulthood. During college, I was not concerned about the loans I owed as I did not even know how much money I had borrowed. Although I was a responsible student, I still was not keeping up with my balances. It was not until after I graduated that I made a plan to pay off all my debt balances. First, I had to get organized by accepting that this money had to be paid back no matter how I felt.

No one makes perfect money decisions all of the time. However, no matter what your situation is, it can be fixed with a plan. The first step is to assess where you are. You must fully embrace your current state and then take charge of your financial health. You have to be very clear about where you are as well as where you want to go.

I know, this may seem like a defeating task if you have not been the most organized with your finances. Many people go day to day without even checking their bank accounts due to lack of interest or fear of the damage they have done. However, money should not be viewed as a monster but as a tool to live life freely.

DEBT IS A MINDSET

Most of the debt you have was the result of your mindset. Look around your house. How many purchased items do you see that used to be "needs?" All that clutter used to be money. Advertisers have programmed many people into subconsciously believing they must have an item they could not afford. Their tactics encourage consumers to buy things with money they do not have. You did not need that credit card. You could have waited and saved before buying that item. Why pay up to 29 percent in interest on a credit card when you could have been earning 12 percent annual returns in the market? "But I need my credit card for emergencies!" That purchase was not an emergency. You just did not prepare for it.

Lenders know most credit card users will forget to pay off their balances every month even when they can afford to do so. Credit cards are not emergency funds. Your own cash should be your emergency fund. You should expect tires to blow, house expenses to occur, a tax bill to be due, and other inconveniences to emerge. You should not hope for an illness or to be laid off, but even these situations should be prepared for. You just lacked patience to build. You did not have to attend that private college. Your local community college or public state colleges provided the same opportunities. You did not need that new car smell; you had a $2,000 car budget. You should have bought the car your bank account said you could afford. You did not need that big house in the suburbs if you could not put down at least 20 percent before acquiring that mortgage. As you can see, most debt is because of lack of savings and patience.

Do not buy into the myth that living paycheck to paycheck is the only way of life. Americans owe around $14 trillion in total debt as only roughly 23 percent of families carry no debt. That means that 77 percent of Americans carry about $137,000 in debt on average per family. This does not have to be you. I know you have heard the phrase, "spend less than you make." But, let us be honest. Is a huge percentage of your paycheck going toward debt payments every month? Does it seem like it is taking forever to pay off debt and that the balances never seem to decrease? If you do not know where to start, you are not alone.

It is time to be realistic and assess where you are. Take a moment to look at what you have spent money on for the last six months. This will tell you everything you need to know about your values. You can do this by running an export of your expenses via online banking. I advise you to use a computer to do this so you can jot down your biggest financial triggers.

Once you have seen your spending habits and trends, label your expenses using these categories:

- Income
- Fixed expenses (any bills)
- Non-fixed expenses (food, shopping, travel, gifts, etc.)
- Debt
- Savings
- Investments (including retirement)
- Insurance
- Miscellaneous (unexpected expenses)

If you find that all of your money is being spent with little money left over to pay off debt and save, it is time to make some changes. We will discuss how to make those changes in Step 3, so for now, just get an understanding of where your money is going.

Next, review your credit report. You can check your credit report for free once a year from all three major credit bureaus at www.annualcreditreport.com. Here, you are not looking for your score, but you are looking for what you legally owe. It is very important to understand the difference between a credit report and a credit score. Credit scores are what lenders provoke you to build in order to remain in debt. The truth is, you only need a clean credit report.

A credit report displays your financial history. This includes: credit cards in your name, mortgages, student loans, personal loans, vehicle loans, public record information, and delinquent debts. This is not the same as a credit score although the two are connected. Do not get hustled by these creditors. Employers and landlords cannot see your actual scores. They can only see your report. The two are not interchangeable. However, your money habits are clearly reflected on your report, which help to calculate your score.

For our purposes, let us only focus on your credit report. A bad credit score is simply a reflection of your personal money habits. It is important to keep your report clean, meaning no negative remarks. The best way to keep your credit report clean is by keeping little to no debt on your report, as well as paying all your bills on time and keeping them out of collections. How does your report look? If it is not what you would like it to be, then keep reading.

Assessing where you are means assessing the people around you. It is really hard to get out of debt if the people around you are influencing you to spend your way back into debt. This makes it even more difficult to build wealth. You know who I am talking about. Those who think they are rich, making you spend money you never budgeted? Those who scream they have money because their credit limit is more than the actual money that they have saved in their bank accounts. Listen, if you have any friends who brag about their credit limits as if that is their actual money, run! Run while on this journey. They cannot help you, and they need to be at a distance in this season. We only want those who will encourage you to do what is right with your finances. Assess your circle.

Stop digging into the hole of debt. If you are close to paying off a credit card, do not rack up more credit card debt on another card. If you are close to paying off a car loan, do not go out and buy a new one. Buying a brand, new car is not smart especially with debt since it depreciates the moment you drive off the lot. Furthermore, buying a used car with a loan is even more unwise. We have to stop going into debt for depreciating assets. That is what we call the broke mentality. Pay in cash or do not buy it.

CAN YOU AFFORD YOUR LIFE?

"If you can't buy it twice, you can't afford

it." This just means, if you have $1,000 in the bank, you really have $500 because you have to prepare for the seen and unseen. If you can buy something twice, then that means you can also handle the upkeep or even replacing it if need be.

Once you have assessed where your financial health is, you can then be honest as to what needs to be done to fix your situation. If we managed our finances like we manage our cell phones or our careers, most people would not be in their current financial state. Yes, you read that correctly. Personal finances should be managed like a job. It takes work and learning the best way to be successful with your finances in order to become financially free. The goal is to control your money and never let it control you. By accepting this challenge to become financially responsible, you are demanding control of your money. And remember, what works for someone else, may not necessarily work for you as personal finance is, well, personal.

It is amazing that we live in a society where we can analyze and piece together everyone else's life but our own. It may seem hard, and I never said it would be easy. Other people's opinions of you do not pay your bills. If it is not beneficial to your wallet, say no. Pretending is expensive, so stop it. We often confuse spending on ourselves with an "I deserve it mentality." We think this will bring happiness, but it is only an escape from a world you are not satisfied with. Escaping your reality is the reason you are in debt. It is time to face you.

The reality is, you are the sum total of all of your financial decisions. If you do not like where you are, only you can change it.

Step 2:

YOUR FINANCIAL STATEMENT

Assets and liabilities should be included in your overall spending plan.

Assets are what is used to create wealth. The assets that increase in value or provide a return are called investments. In other words, assets are what you own such as:

- Cash in savings
- Stocks/investments
- 401k/retirement plans
- Market value of home
- What people owe you

Liabilities are what you owe to others, which is another word for debt. Liabilities include:

- Car loans or leases
- Payday loans
- Credit cards
- Personal loans
- Medical bills
- Mortgages
- 401k loans
- Student loans

There is also a debt that no one really considers: any monthly payment for something that is not a loan with a set price. In other words: apartment leases not paid in full, car insurance, and subscriptions are all liabilities.

If you cannot afford to pay these things in full at once, really consider if the purchase is worth it.

Your net worth will tell you all you need to know about your financial health. Net worth is the difference between assets and liabilities or what you own minus what you owe:

Net worth = Assets - Liabilities

So, when you owe more than you own, your net worth is negative.

The goal of net worth is to be and remain positive. This is what separates the broke from the rich and the rich from the wealthy. To be broke means you are in debt with a negative net worth. To be rich means you can freely buy whatever you want. To be wealthy is to have more than enough resources and assets. Most people buy liabilities that they believe to be assets, which is why they remain broke for so long. If your liabilities amount to more than your assets, do not feel discouraged. This is why this book was written. My goal by the end of this book is to shift your thinking into positive net worth decisions. That can only happen by facing and addressing your financial statement.

When I saw that my net worth was a five-figure negative number, I did not feel good about my financial situation because that meant that I had no money, I just had an income. When we are in debt up to our eyeballs, we tend to trick ourselves into believing that our paychecks are ours. On the contrary, our paychecks belong to the banks until we no longer owe them a balance. No one has money until his or her net worth is positive, which is caused by spending the next two year's income six years ago when you went into debt.

Most people do not realize that having so many liabilities create a sense of urgency in life. An urgency to work every day with the stress of worrying about being fired. The truth of the matter is, most people are one paycheck away from being without comfort, meaning, if they lost their jobs, they would end up being bankrupt and homeless because they do not have enough assets to cover their debts.

This is the reason that I had you assess where you are. In Step 1, you discovered what debts you pay every month, so now you can create another list: a financial statement. In this financial statement, you should list two columns: Assets and Liabilities. Put all your debts into one column and all of your assets into the other column. Before you do this, make sure you are putting actual assets into your column. Many people believe clothes, shoes, furniture, and jewelry to be assets because they spend so much money on them. However, these are all usually depreciating assets and are never worth the same you originally paid for them, if anything at all. I do not include these things into my net worth calculation because I consider assets to be things that build real wealth.

Below is an example of a financial statement for your reference.

NETWORTH STATEMENT

ASSETS	VALUE	LIABILITIES	VALUE
Checking Account (A)	$400	Credit Card (A)	-$800
Checking Account (B)	$200	Credit Card (B)	-$1,200
Savings Account (A)	$2,500	Credit Card (C)	-$6,000
Savings Account (B)	$500	Student Loan	-$50,000
401K Plan	$16,000	Personal Loan	-$8,000
House	$220,000	Mortgage	-$219,000
Car	$20,000	Car Loan	-$15,000
TOTAL ASSETS	$259,600	TOTAL LIABILITIES	-$300,000

NETWORTH	-$40,400

Know what you own and what you owe. There are far too many people walking around with great incomes but high debt and negative net worth. It is time to do better.

Step 3:

CREATE A NEAT SPENDING PLAN

Creating a neat spending plan is simply a plan for how you spend, save, and invest your money. When you have a plan for your money, you are able to build wealth and reach financial freedom because it allows you to be able to understand if you truly can afford the life you choose.

The best way to create a neat spending plan is using your gross income first. Remember, your gross income is what you earn before taxes and deductions. Your net income (take home) is what is left over after taxes and deductions. It is important to know what is coming out of your paycheck before you receive it. You ought to be paying attention to all pre-tax and after tax expenses such as insurance, taxes, and retirement. The wealthy plan according to their gross income.

When creating a neat spending plan, it is best to only plan the consistent income. If you have additional income that is not consistent from month to month, only include it in the plan after it is received. For example, bonuses, overtime, or commission checks, should be included in the neat spending plan for that pay period in which they were received.

Your spending plan should include every single dollar that you earned. One way to ensure that you remain reliant on debt is to never stick to your spending plan. You need to look at your bank account and look at what you spend the most on. Review all of your transactions from the last month, then list all of your expenses and bills to see how much you spent. You will see areas in which you have overspent and can now obtain control in those areas. Allot a certain percentage of income for each category.

WHERE IS MY MONEY GOING?

There are four main categories that most

of our money goes toward each month. This makes us feel as if we are living paycheck to paycheck because we do not plan our spending. Those categories are:

- Rent/Mortgage
- Car/Transportation
- Eating Habits
- Debt

For living expenses, you should separate them from liabilities, there is a difference. You can see them listed below.

Expense: outflow of money to an individual or company as payment for an item or service (utilities, water, phone bill, cable, rent, etc.)

Liability: Debt or money you owe (car note, credit card debt, mortgage, etc.)

There are also two types of expenses: fixed and variable. Fixed expenses are bills you pay regularly, usually the same amount each month (rent, childcare, car insurance). Variable expenses are bills or expenses that vary from month to month (food, clothes, transportation, personal care, gifts). The best way to manage expenses is to cut back on variable spending in order to save.

Try having at least four accounts at three different banks to help manage your money:

- 1 primary checking account for fixed bills at one bank
- 1 checking account for personal and variable expenses at another bank
- 1 account for online savings for emergencies only at separate bank
- 1 account for short term savings/expenses called a buffer at same bank as emergency savings

This will help if you find money planning very exhausting. By automating your bills, savings and fun money in these 4 accounts, you will be better off.

Example:

Your $1300 paycheck is automatically deposited into 4 accounts: $900 in your first checking account to pay bills at Capital One 360, $200 in your second checking account for variable expenses at Charles Schwab Bank, $150 goes toward your savings at Marcus by Goldman Sachs, and $50 goes to your buffer in a separate account at Marcus *by Goldman Sachs.*

This is a way to assure that you do not go over what you have planned for any of these categories. Remember, your emergency savings account should be at a separate bank, preferably online, than both of your checking accounts. You do not want to be tempted to transfer the funds. This will force you to only spend what you have.

LEAVE YOUR PRIMARY ACCOUNT ALONE

A good tip is to not carry a debit card to your primary checking for fixed expenses since that account should be for bills only. Only carry your variable card with you for spending. Your variable card should include your fun/entertainment/personal money. You should always have some cash for your wants so that you do not feel guilty for spending money on personal pleasures. For example, I like to go the hair salon once a week for a conditioning treatment, so I allot the expected amount for that each month while cutting back on other things such as eating out at expensive restaurants. I also allot $50 for personal fun activities, even if I do not use it all that month, but I never go over what I have allotted to spend.

Any time that you need to tap into your emergency fund, make sure to always immediately replenish it, so that you do not have to acquire any new debt. This means that any plans for extra money should be geared toward rebuilding the emergency fund. Some bank recommendations to park your emergency fund are: Ally Bank, Marcus by Goldman Sachs, Capital One or one of your choosing that will allow multiple savings accounts.

Also, your buffer savings are to be used for things such as birthday gifts, giving, annual car maintenance and fees like new car tags or new tires, small household needs, or Christmas gifts. The things that occur every year can be planned for by using a buffer account. A good way to plan for these expenses is to look at the amount you spent on these things the previous year and divide that number by twelve to get your monthly savings number. Make sure you are saving automatically.

You can also create separate savings accounts for different goals or occasional expenses, such as buying a new laptop, car, painting a room, new furniture, or even a new home.

Purchasing a new home is a part of the American Dream for most people, but many people do not understand the financial responsibility and entrapment of a home.

THE TRAP OF THE STARTER HOME

Many people buy a "starter home" to begin their families. However, I hate this term. Why? Because this gives the perception that your first home should not be your desired home. A starter home has trapped many people to a particular location. That is why it is so important to spend a few years planning and designing the home you desire and can actually afford, especially if you plan on growing your family and with the new trend of needing "more space." In fact, according to a recent study conducted by UCLA, majority of Americans only utilize the kitchen, a main room with a television often called a family room, and the bathroom. All other areas, including the deck and porch, go untouched. So really be mindful of the space you claim you need. It might really mean the space you once believed you needed would only be used for more clutter as garages are being used as storage, which means that extra space would be wasted money, especially if you took out a mortgage for the home.

Most people believe that they need a mortgage, but they really just need patience. The truth of the matter is many of the people who live in a house are not homeowners. They are home mortgage renters. This just means that they have taken out a mortgage to be able to live in a house until it is paid off. Meanwhile, the first eight years of the mortgage payments only go toward the interest, so the balance of the loan does not decrease. That is why I teach the possibility of buying a home with cash.

Don't believe that you could buy a home without a mortgage? Let me give you an example. In my home state of Ohio, the average cost of a home is $149,900. By saving $29,980 for five years. You would have enough money to buy the house with cash.

Here is how. If you are a couple and each made $40,000/year or $80,000 together, by living off one income you could easily save $29,980 a year. However, our wants are high and our discipline is few, thus, we take on many financial detriments that turn into obligations that take most of our paychecks each and every month. This is often in the form of debt, much of what was never needed in the first place. Just imagine not even having at least half of the debt you have, what could you be doing with just half?

If you are single, your aim for paying with cash should be to save at least half of the price of the home. If your average salary was $50,000/year. You could save $15,500 for five years and have more than enough for a great down payment. This goal is hard to accomplish with debt and living above one's means.

Also, by waiting and looking for a few years to buy a home, you are more prone to buy a home you actually love and will not have to worry about moving because you do not actually like your kitchen design after two years of living there. Sacrifice does not mean living below your means, sacrifice means going without all of your wants until you have the means. It means telling yourself no while society is giving you every reason to tell yourself yes.

You see, society has focused so much on credit scores that it has forced us to believe we cannot afford anything without one. However, we can, just not everything at once. This is why it is so important to rid yourself of consumer debt prior to buying a home, so you can save up for the house you need, not just a home you think you want. Do not rush homeownership, seven years may seem like an eternity, but the wait will be worth it. I say seven years because it should take no more than two years to pay off consumer debt and five years to save up and research for your home.

The only thing standing in your way is you. This also means you must have the right income for the house you need, not the right debt for the house you want. If you cannot afford to save for a house, you cannot afford a house in the first place. Do not let your friends, family, neighbors, coworkers, or society speed you up to buy a home before your bank account and your reality affords you that opportunity.

If you cannot sacrifice for a few years, an average mortgage is for you.

HOW TO BUY A MORTGAGE

I will tell you the smartest way to purchase a home if you plan on buying a mortgage because most people confuse the two. Buying a house means you own it, with no debt attached to it. Buying a mortgage means that you are renting the house from a bank that owns it. Here are the basic steps for smart home buying:

1. All of your high interest consumer debt is paid off (credit cards, payday loans, personal loans).
2. Paying 12 to 24 months on similar installment loans (car loan and student loans) to establish payment history.
3. Have a 4 to 6 month emergency fund.
4. Save up at least 20 percent for the down payment.
5. Calculate the interest paid for a conventional 15-year fixed versus a conventional 30-year fixed mortgage (I recommend going with the 15-year fixed if you plan on living in your house more than 15 years).
6. The total mortgage is not more than 2.5 times your annual gross salary (lenders may approve you for up to 5 times your annual salary, do not take on that financial burden).

Contrary to popular belief, opening up new credit cards or buying a new car right before you buy a home will hurt your chances of getting approved for a mortgage loan. Lenders are looking at your income as well as your debt levels. The ideal number for debt to income ratio (percentage of gross income going to debt payments) is to stay below thirty-six percent.

If all of the above seems implausible, you are not ready to be a homeowner. In addition to the mortgage payment, you must consider the additional expenses that come with buying a home whether you have a mortgage or not: property taxes, repairs, yard maintenance, roof maintenance, higher electricity and water, furnishing the house (the bigger the house, the more money you waste on senseless items bought with credit cards), and plumbing. Remember, there is no landlord. So, the phrase, "I pay so much for rent! I will save money by buying a house," is a myth for many. Expect for something to always need attention or repairing. Do the math and you will be fine. Do not do that math and you may just spend two to three times more on the house than it cost you. The choice is yours. I do not say this to try to dissuade you from buying a home, but to show that buying a home takes a lot more than worrying about if you can afford the mortgage. Affording a mortgage does not mean you can afford the house.

YOUR BIGGEST EXPENSE THAT IS REALLY HURTING YOU

There is only so much you can do to

decrease your expenses. Want to know what will really help you with your finances? Cutting back on your rent. This is usually one's largest expense and most likely, an expense that is above what he or she should be paying. Your rent should be 25 percent or less of your gross monthly income. If you are spending more than this, chances are, you are house poor. In addition, your utilities should be between 3-5 percent of your monthly gross income. The two combined should be up to 30 percent max, especially during your wealth building phase. Paying more than this per month means that you cannot afford other things. This is the biggest saver, even if you spend $400 on food, if you focused on decreasing your rent, there is a better chance of getting out of debt or saving than just focusing on cooking and eating out. Here are some options to help lower this category:

- Rent until you can afford a house.
- Live with a roommate and decrease expenses by half until you are financially stable.
- Live with a partner, but do not combine accounts unless married, just split expenses; but if you are married, combine incomes and plan

that way (dual income is best way for anyone to build wealth).

- Live with family, this could mean paying no rent, which is ideal for singles paying off massive amounts of debt.

Example:

Your income is $2,200 per month, and your current rent is $700 for a one-bedroom, one-bath apartment. Your utilities on average cost you roughly $150 per month. Your Wi-Fi costs you $50 per month. You are already spending $900 per month before you can even address other expenses, savings and debt payments.

Remember, the $2,200 per month is your gross, which means, your actual take home pay is more like $1,800 per month. Your car note is $300 per month. Your car insurance is $200 per month. Your student loan payment is $150 per month. This leaves you with $240, you still need groceries ($100), gas ($100), savings ($40), phone bill (-$60) and anything extra that might come up.

How in the world can you get ahead or enjoy some of your money if you are living paycheck to paycheck? You can't.

This is why while you are in the debt payoff phase and wealth-building phase, you must have help. Say you get a roommate for a two-bedroom apartment for $1,000 per month and this cuts your rent by $200 per month and your expenses can vary, but the average is $200 per month, your payment is cut by $50. Your Wi-Fi is cut by $25, so now you have an additional $275 per month.

You have options now that your expenses have been decreased. You can use that extra money to cover your $60 per month phone bill and pay off debt quicker. Or, if you have no consumer debt, you could just save that entire $275 per month, which would be $16,500 after five years or pay extra toward student loans. You could also use this extra cash to invest and after five years, you would have approximately $19,763 in investments (with an average rate of return of 8 percent).

All it takes is short-term sacrifice and

discipline. This is why it is recommended to buy a home after consumer debts are paid. Renting does not need to be permanent, but if you can sacrifice for a few years, your future self will thank you. This includes avoiding rent-to-own homes.

TRUE COST OF YOUR CAR

In addition to your rent, your car expenses can hurt you, especially if you have a car note with a high interest rate. The fact of the matter is, unless you do not have a car, you will always have a form of a car payment. However, it is a choice to always have a car note. What is the difference you ask? Car payments are the costs of having a car: gas, insurance, repairs, newer car, parking, car detailing, etc. Car notes are what you owe on the car you are in debt for. It is a liability that depreciates, which you pay for as well. However, when you purchase a car in full, it will cost you less over time. Most people who take out a loan for a car, have an interest rate between 2-13 percent, anything above that is robbery and you do not need that car. You definitely should not be purchasing a car that is more than 1/3 of your annual gross salary.

Moreover, the average car note is $531 per

month for about 72 months for a new car.

The best way to purchase a car until you have built up a positive and firm sitting net worth, is to pay cash for a used vehicle. You should never buy a brand-new car (two years or older), and if you are considering a lease, don't. However, if you are debt free and receive enough money in earnings from your investments, a brand-new car is more feasible, but until then, buy used cars with cash.

In addition, the average car maintenance will cost you roughly $1,200 per year. Gas can range from $1,000 to $3,000 per year. Insurance can range from $1,000 to $2,500 depending on your driving history. Thus, a car can cost you an additional $6,700 at minimum a year without adding in a car note or other car expenses. This is why I am against anyone having a car note. Many millionaires even claim that using public transportation is best rather than buying a car because of the annual costs. However, it has become such an acquired necessity that this is unlikely to happen for most. So, use apps like GasBuddy, which shows you the gas prices at any local gas station no matter your location, to save on gas. Rent out a car you do not use often on sites like Turo.com (similar to Airbnb). Buy fuel efficient cars. Do whatever you can to save.

GET RID OF THE CAR NOTE FOR GOOD

Let's use the average car note of about $500 per month. Create a "Car Payment Savings Account" and pay yourself $500 per month (helps to avoid interest and cannot be reported on your credit report if you "miss" a payment) car payment for seven months, that will give you $3,500, and if you are truly patient and wait 12 months, you will have $6,000. Buy a used, reliable car (I recommend Toyotas and Hondas for this price), including the taxes, and have no car note.

Next, instead of saving $500 per month, decrease this to $250 per month for 3-5 years. This could be between $9,000 to $15,000 to buy a better, reliable used car. Then, you can sell your car as a private seller, not to a dealer, for $2,000 to $4,000, depending on the condition (use Kelley Blue Book to get an estimate of your car). Combine this with your savings, and you can purchase a very nice, used car in cash every 5-10 years or even longer. This should also decrease your insurance since you actually own the car and not the bank.

THOSE WHO STILL PREFER CAR NOTES

For those who cannot stay away from car notes, and do not mind the negative equity you are paying double for due to your credit score not being "good," this is for you. Even if you have a high credit score, this is also for you. Go to a credit union prior to purchasing the car and open up an account. Ask the lender which credit score (ex. TransUnion or Equifax) they use prior to financing the car. Put money in a savings account, this can be started with your tax refunds as long as you have paid off some debt and saved most of it and add an additional $200 per month for 6-8 months. Then start looking for a used car. Once you have found the car you want (no more than 1/3 of your annual gross salary) and you have 50 to 90 percent of the price of the car saved up in cash, go to the dealership after being approved for a loan by the credit union. Credit unions usually have better interest rates than the ones the dealership may say "approved" you especially if this is your first car loan and you have minimal or no payment history for installment loans. Take the car for an inspection and then aim to negotiate. Do not let your interest rate go above 10 percent. If so, you should not buy that car and should buy a reliable hooptie instead. Then pay off the car as early as possible in a lump sum if possible.

YOUR EATING HABITS

The average millennial spends $526 per month or $6,316 per year on food. This does not include the amount spent on alcohol, which is an additional $500 per year.

How do you decrease your spending on food? Start assigning an amount or percentage of income to not go over. For example, you can create a weekly plan to stay under $50 per week on food spending. Or you can try keeping the amount spent on food (groceries and eating out) to 12 percent or less of your take home pay until you are debt free. After that, you can increase to 15 percent as long as you are investing and saving more.

For a family, a good goal may be to spend about $30 a week per family member. This will help when meal planning and sticking to a spending plan. By setting a limit per family member, this will also cause you to make or purchase meals that will last longer than one day.

You do not think it matters? Let's do the math. Say you eat out for lunch and dinner every day because you do not make time to cook or pack your lunch. You spend $10 on lunch and $10 on dinner on average during the week. On the weekends, you get a little fancier and spend an average of $70 between Friday night and Sunday. This equals $160 per week on just one person, this does not even include if you have a family. A family of five could easily amount to $500 a week on food without preparation or $26,000 a year.

Once you truly become intentional, you can plan to not go over $50 a week on food, which is a decrease of $110 per week. This means an additional $110 per week or $5,720 a year to save, pay off debt, or invest. That extra $110 per week could almost max out a Traditional or Roth IRA (discussed in Step 9) that would be worth over $419,000 in 25 years using an average annual return of 8 percent. This is why it is important to meal plan.

COOKING IS NOT FOR ME

If you are always in a rush and never have

time to cook or do not know how to cook, do not buy groceries. Only buy essentials like fruit and some beverages to keep around the house. Use that money to eat out or buy prepared meals instead after you create a meal plan for your weekly meals. Being on the go is not an excuse to overspend on food. You can go to stores that offer cooked food like Meijer or Whole Foods and stock up for a few days at a time. There is nothing wrong with not cooking as long as you are spending within your allotted limit.

Also, learn how to restaurant hack. By restaurant hacking, you will save money on buying food. Download restaurant apps on your phone, sign up for coupons, order a cup of water instead of bottled water or a fountain drink. If you have children, go to restaurants where children eat free or at a discount on certain nights.

There are several ways to save money even when you do not cook, you need to be intentional with your food spending plan, do not just swipe your card. Plan out every meal so that you do not go over what is allotted for your food spending. However, eating out is not an excuse for not eating healthy. Make sure you are not consuming food that causes you not to take care of your body because that will cause other financial issues.

FOR THOSE WHO WILL COOK

If you do cook, start looking at alternative grocery stores such as Aldi until you can afford to shop at a more expensive grocery store. Start meal planning on the weekends and do not go shopping without a list or on an empty stomach. If you meal plan, you are more likely to spend less and create meals that last for more than one day.

WHAT IF I DON'T HAVE STEADY INCOME

The good news is, the spending philosophy still works for you too! Your fixed expenses will not change from month to month, so as long as you have enough to deposit into your primary checking where your fixed expenses are assigned to go, you will be just fine. For your variable checking account, that may change from month to month, but the good news is, you are the one who controls this. However, it may be good to look at what you have earned within the past six months and look at your lowest paycheck. Once you have seen your lowest paycheck, plan as if that is the expected amount you will receive each month and then anything above that should go to variable expenses. If you find that your lowest paycheck would not cover your fixed expenses, then you may need to increase your overall income. Also, if you are spending too much on wants, it may be time to decrease what you are spending.

Step 4:

DECREASE YOUR EXPENSES

It is very important to understand how decreasing expenses help your overall spending plan and goals. By looking at the things we spend our money on, we are able to see that many of the things we once thought was important are no longer of relevance in our lives. It is also important to understand the things you value. If you do not have this understanding, you will continue to pay for expenses that keep you broke and bound to working for your entire life. By decreasing your expenses, you now have extra money to start attacking your goals with aggression.

Below are some of the ways that you can immediately decrease your expenses:

- Reduce your rent
- Eliminate monthly bills; pay bills in full or get rid of them
- Sell your car
- Use public transportation
- Stop going out every weekend
- Stop shopping for clothes and shoes
- Reduce childcare
- Reduce extracurricular activities for your kids
- Lower your cell phone bill or switch providers
- Reduce your car insurance
- Buy generic brands
- Buy luxury coffee such as Starbucks twice a week instead of every day
- Be selective with eating out by planning your weekly meals
- Cancel unused subscriptions
- Eliminate cable
- Decrease traveling
- Look for low cost or free fun activities
- Cancel gym membership
- Request credit card rate reduction

- Cut back on grooming and beauty regimen, especially hair and make up
- Use cash or a prepaid card when out instead of a debit card
- Get rid of bad habits like smoking
- Give away or sell your pet
- Get an accountability partner to make sure you stick to your spending plan
- Wait 24 to 72 hours before buying any impulse purchases
- Decrease your time on social media watching other people spend money they do not have

Another recommendation that I share to help cut expenses is to temporarily stop any type of investing. The main type of investment that many people have is their employer sponsored retirement plan. If you are under the age of 45, you can afford to pause your retirement investments on a temporary basis until you figure out a plan. If you are above the age of 45, you should not stop retirement investing, but you should lower your contributions to the employer match or decrease by 50 percent until you are out of consumer debt. This helps you to have more disposable income to go toward your short-term goals of eliminating debt, which will be discussed more in depth in Step 5.

If you have any other form of investing, temporarily pause those as well. It makes no sense to invest if you have consumer debt because you are losing money. It only takes 24 months to 36 months to get completely out of consumer debt if you have the right plan. Once you have gotten out of consumer debt, you can contribute to any type of investment that you had before as long as you have enough disposable income to attack the rest of your debts if you have them. These other debts would include student loans and a mortgage. If you do not have these two types of loans, then this does not apply to you.

YOUR CREDIT SCORE

You have hundreds of credit scores, not only the three many believe there are. So, you actually never know the credit score a lender will use. However, third party sites like Credit Karma and Credit Sesame will provide you with your consumer education scores, which means an idea of where you currently stand. These third-party sites employ a different scoring method called the VantageScore, which provides you with a score that is a small percentage of your FICO credit score, which stands for Fair Isaac Corporation, but it will not be the FICO credit score your lenders will likely use. Your VantageScore also shows utility bills.

Creditors know that many people rely on these third-party VantageScores and market to consumers with headliners claiming what credit cards and lines of credit you could be approved for.

The main credit score used by lenders is one of your FICO credit scores. Your credit score is broken down into five components:

- ➢ 35% Payment History
- ➢ 30% Amounts Owed
- ➢ 15% Length of Credit History
- ➢ 10% Credit Mix
- ➢ 10% New Credit

I do not recommend using any form of credit, but I understand the weight it carries in many people's lives. If you are bad with money, you should not be focusing on credit anyway.

What good is having a 700+ credit score when you are drowning in debt only making the minimum payments and do not even have $700 in a savings account, or worse, a negative net worth?

I am sharing some tips to have a good FICO credit score in addition to good money habits in order to help decrease high interest rate loans and predatory lending for when you choose to take out a loan for cars and homes only. Taking out a loan for any other reason is not smart. For the purposes of this section, credit score will be used interchangeably with FICO credit score.

BUILDING YOUR CREDIT SCORE

If you want to build or improve your FICO credit score, you must understand what positively and negatively impacts your credit score. As I stated previously, you have several credit scores, so the one you need to build should be the focus at the time you are taking out a specific loan.

Remember, a credit score only affects your ability to qualify for different types of credit and interest rates. A credit score is not a qualifier of your success if you are actually good with money and want to be debt free.

The truth is, nobody needs a credit score. Many believe that financing items is the only way to afford it. So, this section is for those who want to borrow money in the smartest way possible.

You never really want to have more than five types of lines of credit on your report. You also never want to have multiple credit cards, no more than two to be safe.

Contrary to popular belief, you do not even need a credit card to build your credit score. In fact, if your goal is to buy an auto loan or a mortgage, a credit card is a different type of loan not necessary to build your Fico credit scores for auto lending and mortgage lending.

A credit card is a revolving loan, which means you do not have a fixed repayment plan, and it can be renewed each time the balance is paid off. A student loan, car loan, private personal loan, or mortgage is an installment loan, which means you do have a fixed, periodic repayment plan with a lender, and it is closed after it is repaid.

Revolving credit can be more dangerous than installment credit because the creditor can change interest rates if there is a missed or late payment. Revolving credit also often comes in the form of really high interest rates with the average interest rate being 16.2 percent.

However, there may be drawbacks to repaying installment loans as well. Some installment loan repayment plans penalize you for making extra payments. So, make sure that you understand your loan agreement and how you are to make extra debt payments, especially for auto loans and mortgages. Contact your lenders before making any extra payments.

Here is how to build your credit score for credit cards and revolving credit loans:

➢ Apply for a secured credit card if you are building from scratch and then once you have built some credit, you may be able to apply for another card with little to no annual fees.

➢ Only utilize up to 30% of the balance allotted to you each month, and never go above this.

➢ Pay 100% of the balance used that month.

➢ Never open more than 2 cards and do not have too many open accounts on your credit report.

> Always check your scores and reports annually.

If keeping a revolving credit score is important to you, then you have to have self-control. By self-control, I mean, you must pay the balance off each month and never max out your credit cards or get behind on payments. After 90 days, most lenders will report your delinquent payments to a collection agency. So, if you have trouble, make sure you reach out to a lender.

WHAT HAPPENS WHEN A CREDIT CARD IS PAID OFF

A way to keep your card active without going back into debt is to buy a cup of coffee with the card twice a month and then pay it off before the grace period ends for that month. The goal is to always keep your credit utilization rate between 7-30 percent; anything higher means that you are using too much of other people's money and you have a spending problem. A good rule to stand by is to never buy anything with a credit card that you cannot pay for with cash.

BUILDING YOUR CREDIT FOR INSTALLMENT LOANS

Only a small portion of your credit score is based on revolving credit, which is usually in the form of credit cards. This is why opening credit cards are not necessary for building the credit scores you will need to obtain an auto loan or mortgage loan.

I say this from experience. I have never had any form of revolving credit, but I did have an installment loan in the form of student loans. Having student loans and paying it on time boosted my FICO credit score and VantageScore into the 700s, according to my third-party reports.

If you have student loans, this is another great way to build your installment credit. By paying your student loans, especially if you plan to take the long route of 10 years of consecutive payments, you will prove to lenders that you are a responsible borrower. Since payment history makes up 35% of your credit score, paying this consistently for a period of time will build the credit you need. Because this is an installment loan, paying your student loans is enough to increase your score within a range that will enable you to apply for another installment loan such as a mortgage or auto loan.

Another way is to simply pay off current debts. By paying off your debts, you will decrease your debt to income ratio while also establishing positive payment history. Please, never be a co-signer for anyone with a low credit score nor someone else trying to build credit. This is one of the worst financial decisions you could do.

Lenders also take a look into your income and other debts when making decisions to lend money as well as the interest rates. So, if your income is low, you may be more prone to predatory lending (being charged very high interest rates).

Also, if you do not have student loans, you may report your rental payments to your credit reports for rental history by asking your landlord to submit your payments to a credit agency or you can sign up with a third-party rent reporter. Again, this shows your payment history, which is the bulk of your credit score. This will not affect your FICO credit score, but this can boost your VantageScore consumer credit.

The last option would be to take out a small private, personal loan of no more than $2,000 and repay it over time, the earlier you pay it off, the better.

If you are trying to qualify for a bigger auto loan, you can buy a used, reliable car that is no older than ten years old and have at minimum 80 percent of the down payment, then pay off the remaining 20 percent balance. For example, a used 2009, Toyota Corolla ranges between $5,000 to $9,000 before taxes and fees. If you have 80 percent of the down payment in cash, the car salesman would probably be more willing to negotiate for a lower price. So, offer a total price of $7,000 including taxes and fees. An 80 percent down payment for that would be $5,600. That would leave you with a balance of $1,400. Pay this off within six to twelve months.

If you do happen to finance anything, do not close any cards or open any new cards or other loans 6-12 months prior to financing. Multiple inquiries at one time or within a short period of time will hurt your credit scores.

If you default on your loans, this will hurt your chances of getting approved for any hardship programs as well as any government sponsored programs. Wage garnishment is one way that lenders will get their money back. Some lenders may even sue you. Being sued depends on the statute of limitations for your state, which could be up to fifteen years in some states after the last loan payment was made.

Overall, my motto still stands; the best way to purchase anything is with patience and cash.

Step 5:

RAISE YOUR
INCOME

There are only so many ways that you can decrease your expenses. Now, it is time to think about increasing your income. There are many ways that you can increase your income without necessarily over working your body.

Not only is it important to increase your income to pay off debt, but it is also important to increase your income in general. The average millionaire has three sources of income. Within those sources, they have seven streams of income. Having one source is almost like gambling because if you lose your job, you risk diving into debt. By diversifying your sources of income and adding income producing streams, you have other options to get paid.

The main sources of income are earned, passive, and residual. Earned income requires you to do some work in order to be paid. Passive income requires only capital and then your money will begin to grow on its own so long as it is invested in income producing assets such as stocks, real estate, or equity within a company. Residual income comes from creating a product or idea once and then you receive payments from doing the work one time. This income is often in the form of books, royalties, or a product. It is good to have all three sources and then create streams within those sources. For example, if you have a full-time job and a side hustle of cutting grass, you have earned income. Both would be the same source but different streams. Having a second source would be writing a book and having it sell over and over again, this would be residual. Whatever you decide to do, understand increasing and diversifying your income is no longer a choice, but a necessity.

MORE INCOME CREATES OPTIONS

By increasing your income by $100-$1,000 a month, you could quickly change the trajectory and timeframe of your release from your debt prison sentence.

A side hustle is simply any type of job that is done in addition to your full-time job. Many side hustles can turn into a job for people who enjoy doing what they do on the side, however, the main reason for the side hustle in this season of your life is to help accelerate your goals.

For example, I had two side hustles while getting out of debt that enabled me to earn enough money to pay for my variable expenses. This meant that I was able to devote my main paycheck and source of income to my future financial goals.

While I was paying off my debt balance, I decided to get a job doing something that I love to do. I looked up jobs on Indeed.com for opportunities working with children. I applied to jobs that allowed me to work in the nursery at a church. After I was hired, I was able to work as the Nursery Coordinator for a church in the morning before my home church's service began. That turned into additional weekly hours. By doing this, I was able to increase my monthly income by $200 to $400 per month. I then decided to babysit one to two weekends out of each month, which added an additional $50 to $100 per month.

When I realized that I could do all my fun activities with this side hustle money, I was able to use my actual job to pay for my other expenses and goals. Think of it this way, if you increase your income enough to cover your largest expense, or maybe just a couple hundred of dollars per month, you will see the effect the extra money will have not only for your current position but also your future. With this side hustle money, I did not have to give up my fun and things that I enjoyed just to focus on my goals only. This increased my intensity to pay off my debt. By getting this side hustle, I was able to triple my minimum payment for my debt, which gave me even more momentum to get rid of debt faster. My side hustle only took about 4 to 6 hours a week. It was a small sacrifice to get out of debt without depriving myself.

Some people are not willing to sacrifice a few extra hours per week doing something that will benefit them in the long term. You cannot complain about your income and do nothing to change it. Side hustles are some of the quickest ways to increase your income, and they are easier to obtain now more than ever.

I often tell my clients to get a side hustle to either help pay for expenses so that they can save more money or pay off debt quicker. For example, say your car note is roughly $400 a month, if you get a side hustle that earns at least $400 a month, you can double your payment for that car note or you can use that additional $400 to 1) pay off your other debt or 2) save more money. However, by doubling your debt payment each month, you decrease the amount of interest that you will pay over time, which causes you to save more money to be able to pursue your freedom and your dreams.

Here are some suggestions in order to find a side hustle that works for you or ways to earn more money each paycheck.

- Go on Indeed.com and search for part time jobs or something in your field
- Start a home-based side hustle that allows you to build up a clientele to sell your products to
- Maximize any hobbies, skills, or talents you have (i.e. musicians can play or teach music, financial coaching, cleaning services,

babysitting, dog walking, cutting grass, shoveling snow, selling old items you no longer use, etc)
- Freelance or contract positions
- Work from home data entry jobs
- Tutoring/Adjunct Instructor
- Ask for over-time hours at your current job
- Change your W4 withholdings, especially when receiving a raise by going to an HR representative any time throughout the year. Visit irs.gov to see what amount you should withhold from your check for state and federal taxes
- Switch to banks that offer no fee minimum accounts (Charles Schwab, credit unions, Capital One 360, Ally Bank, Fidelity Cash Management)

Remember, do what is hard now so that you are not doing what is harder later. By simply doing what is most beneficial for your bank accounts today, your future self will be rewarded for your discipline, time, effort, and sacrifice to build. Even if your side hustle produces inconsistent income, create a monthly goal minimum of income to make and you will be just fine.

IT MAY BE TIME TO MOVE ON

In addition to getting a side hustle, it may be time for a career change or to find a new employer. When looking for a new job, aim to seek an income increase of 10 to 20 percent. By switching employers, you are more likely to obtain a higher salary than by staying at the same company.

ASK FOR A RAISE

In addition, if changing employers is not ideal, it may be time to ask for a raise or promotion. Only do this if you have been at your current company for at least 18 months. It is important to have written documentation displaying a track record of results and accomplishments within your department. You can research what salary you should be expected to be paid based on your education and experience by going to PayScale.com or Glassdoor.com. Just put in all of your information in regard to what you have done and compare it to those with similar backgrounds and experience.

THE IMPORTANCE OF NEGOTIATION

Learn how to negotiate! By negotiating for

a better salary anytime you ask for a raise or get a new job, you need to truly negotiate. By not negotiating your salary, you could be leaving up to an additional $7,538 or at least 13 percent more on the table per year according to Glassdoor. What could you do with an additional $7,538 a year? Some quick tips on how to earn a higher salary:

1. Know your value. As mentioned previously, PayScale and Glassdoor will give you an honest evaluation of your value for your education and experience in the market.
2. Make sure your resume and cover letter present all of your results not just a list of responsibilities. What makes you stand out?
3. Never state your current salary to a new employer.
4. Never be the first to address salary in an interview.
5. Research the position and salary expectations for the position in your field and region.
6. Always respond to any salary questions with, *I am looking to be paid between $xx and $xx based on my education and skill set.*
7. Understand compensation is more than what you are paid. Consider vacation, health insurance, and

benefits because all of these things affect your income as well.

Those who do negotiate boost their starting salaries by $5,000 on average according to a study published by the Journal of Organizational Behavior. That additional $5,000 could be used to pay off debt, save, or invest.

NEED MORE?

Additionally, one way to increase your income is to temporarily stop contributing to your employer sponsored retirement plans. If you are under the age of 45 years old, you can sacrifice contributing to your retirement plan or any other form of investments for 24 months. Or, you can temporarily stop until your consumer debt is paid. If it will not take you 24 months to get completely out of consumer debt, then you do not have to wait that long. The average person takes about 24 to 36 months to get out of consumer debt. If you only have student loans and a mortgage, and possibly a car payment with an interest rate of less than 5%, then you should not stop contributing to your retirement plans. If you need to free up more money, then it makes sense to temporarily stop even if you have no consumer debt until you understand how to get your spending plan in order.

If you are over the age of 45, then we really have to consider whether temporarily stopping your retirement contributions is a smart overall plan depending on your retirement goals. If you plan on retiring at the age of 65, then maybe 24 months of sacrifice will not harm you. By sacrifice I mean, splitting your current contribution by half. For example, if you are contributing 5 percent to your retirement account, cut it down to 2.5 percent for the time you are paying off consumer debt. Then you can increase it back to 5 percent after consumer debt is paid off. If you cannot afford to contribute to your retirement account and make additional payments to your debt, then temporarily stop contributing for three months until you find extra amounts of disposable income that will replace the money that is going into your retirement account. For example, if you are contributing 5% of your income toward your retirement, and temporarily stop contributing that 5%, find out what the 5% is. When you find out what that 5% is, see if you can find a side hustle that will pay you the same amount so that you can then begin to contribute to your retirement again. Time is of the essence in the market, so you do not want to take away your retirement.

It is a personal decision to temporarily pause your retirement contributions. This decision should be made after consulting your financial planner, financial coach, or financial advisor. After that consultation, do your own calculations so you are clear on how much money you need to retire comfortably. I say age 45 because you still have at least 20 years until retirement. However, if you are 60, then it does not make any sense to stop contributing. Again, this is a personal decision based on your age and number that you have in retirement during debt elimination phase.

THE POWER OF DUAL INCOME

Lastly, a great way to increase your income is to work with your spouse or partner. By working on a financial plan together as a team, your income will greatly increase. Team work is truly dream work, if you create your financial plan that will help you, not only for the short term, but the long term as well. You never want to be the reason your household is not winning financially. Who you marry is highly connected to your financial success, so you should be able to trust your partner to help you when combining finances and decisions, not force you to handle the financial burdens alone. If you cannot trust your partner with the finances, you have bigger problems than just financial. This is why it is good to have intentional and serious financial conversations prior to marriage to understand how finances will be handled during the marriage (ask about income, debts, credit reports, spending plans, kids, housing, etc.).

Discuss all major financial decisions together. Never hide any purchases from your spouse or partner. That leads to financial infidelity, which means you can no longer be trusted with finances. Every couple ought to have personal, guilt free spending accounts, however, any other decisions should be decided together.

Make a decision to never borrow money from friends or family, especially without discussing with your partner. Also, never lend money to friends or family. If you want to help, give them what you truly can afford and expect nothing in return.

Furthermore, learn to live on one income. Living off two will lead to financial disaster especially if one of you loses a job. That way, it is easier to pay off debt and invest later.

Finances is the number one cause of divorce. If you are dating and the person does not show signs of changing bad financial habits, this is a red flag that they may never change. Whoever told you that you cannot plan a marriage lied to you.

Having a financial plan prior to getting married should be mandatory. This ensures that the two of you are on the same page and that there are no surprises in the future, this includes the costs of having children. (Children are expected to cost roughly $20,000 in the first year alone). Make sure that this is all discussed so that the two of you can work on a plan together. Divorces are expensive and preventable. Do not spend more time planning the wedding than you do planning the marriage.

Step 6:

SAVE ONE MONTH OF FIXED EXPENSES OR $2,000

Did you know only 60 percent of Americans can cover a $400 emergency? That is because most people do not strategically plan to set-aside money for unexpected expenses. Although, every year, something unplanned is bound to happen. But because of the "safety net" of credit cards, payday loans, personal loans, or family, many people do not plan for the future.

As we discussed in Step Five, increasing your income is very crucial to accelerating your goals. If you find that you cannot save money, that means that you also cannot pay extra on debt payments. Now it should be evident that you do have an income problem and need to increase your income. After you find your desired approach to increase your income, make sure that you have the appropriate savings that you need before making extra debt payments.

A simple way to do this is to open up a savings account at an online bank or at a bank that is separate from your personal checking account. This was also mentioned in Step Three, which talked about creating a spending plan.

One thing that I have learned by working with people and many studies that I have read is that automation creates a new type of behavior that manual transfers do not. If you automatically transfer money on payday from your actual paycheck to your savings account, you will not even notice that it was never there to spend in the first place. By having savings at a separate bank, you will also not be tempted to use the money for savings for other things that are not necessary.

THE STARTER EMERGENCY FUND

I have a philosophy that most people need at minimum $2,000 saved in case of an emergency at all times while paying off consumer debt. Another way to plan for an emergency is to at least have all your fixed expenses saved in an emergency fund. For example, I mentioned that most fixed expenses are the basic necessities you need to live. So, if you have at least one month of fixed expenses saved, you could use that to pay for an unexpected life event. This simply means that you have money set aside to at least cover your rent or mortgage, utilities, car insurance, car payment, or any other bill that is necessary in a savings account. So, that would look something like this:

- Rent/Mortgage: $1,200
- Utilities: $200
- Car Insurance: $200
- Phone Bill: $100
- Car payment: $400

These expenses equal $2,100. Understand that building adequate savings will take some time for the majority of people. You must be patient to have the desired amount in your savings account.

NO MORE CREDIT CARDS

As mentioned previously, getting a side hustle can accelerate your savings goals so that you can start eliminating debt. You are not to make extra debt payments until you have an emergency fund. The emergency fund is so you do not dig yourself deeper into debt. Not having an adequate emergency fund is the reason why 40 percent of Americans cannot cover a $400 emergency and 60 percent cannot cover a $1,000 emergency. Become your own credit card so that you never have to rely on one again.

Step 7:

CREATE A DEBT PAY OFF PLAN

The average monthly debt payments including the mortgage, student loans, car note and credit cards, equal approximately $2,000. Remember, this is only making the minimum payments.

Imagine that instead of paying this much in debt payments each month, you invested this $2,000 per month in your early retirement investments for 25 years. This would be $1,768,239.51 using an average return of 8 percent.

TRUTH ABOUT MINIMUM PAYMENTS

Minimum payments will keep you in debt. Making minimum payments is never to assist you in paying off debt, it is only for the lender to make its money. The lender makes so much money off of the interest you pay per month. This makes paying more than the minimum payment a wise choice to get out of debt faster. You read above that your money could be working for you, compounding over time with an average return of 5-8 percent yet instead of this, when you are paying debt and interest, your money is working against you.

Example:

You have a credit card that gave you a limit of $2,000 with an interest rate of 16 percent. You spend $1,200 on furniture. Since most lenders allow you to only pay 3 percent of the balance, you only pay $36/month. This will take you 45 months to pay off if you only paid the minimum balance with $397.64 going to interest. Let's say you doubled your monthly payment on a biweekly basis and added an additional $36 per month. This *would decrease your payments to 19 months with $166.14 going to interest. This is why it is always good to pay more than the minimum.*

I know what you are thinking, *well what if I have multiple debts and can only afford to make the minimums to each*? Here are the options you should consider while also making sure that any extra debt payments go to the principal and not the interest:

Debt Snowball: Listing all your debts from the smallest balance to highest balance, no matter the interest rate of each, and paying the minimum balance of all except the smallest. Pay as much as you can on the smallest debt. When you have paid off the smallest debt, add that payment to the next smallest debt. Repeat this cycle for each debt. This builds momentum and is the recommended strategy for beginning to pay off debt.

Debt Avalanche: Listing all your debts from highest to lowest interest rate. Pay as much toward the debt with the highest interest rate while making minimum payments on the other debts. When you have paid off the first debt, add that payment the next highest interest debt. This might be a quicker way to getting out of debt.

Debt Snowflake: This is a pay-off plan if you do not have a minimum or maximum extra monthly payment on a steady plan. A snow flake can be an extra payment toward a debt whenever you receive some extra cash. Every little bit helps when it comes to eliminating debt.

Below is an example of a debt repayment plan using the snowball method.

DEBT SNOWBALL CALCULATOR

Creditor	Balance	Rate	Min. Payment	Repayment Order
Auto Loan #1	$3,200.00	9.81%	$30.00	1
Credit Card	$4,400.00	13.00%	$50.00	2
Auto Loan #2	$5,000.00	12.00%	$55.00	3
Student Loan #1	$9,500.00	4.75%	$143.85	4
Student Loan #2	$21,200.00	4.75%	$262.12	5
	$43,200.00		$540.97	

Here, you are shown all debts listed with the interest rates and minimum payments. It is up to you to decide how much you need to pay extra each month to pay off your debts by a certain time. You need to decide what date you want to be debt free and according to that date, figure out how much extra you should pay toward debt each month.

For example, using the list above, if you

want to be debt free by December 2022 with your payment plan beginning in August 2019, you would need to pay a total of $1,200 a month, which would be a snowball of an additional $659.03 per month on top of your minimum payments until December 2022. You must create a concrete and written down plan to attack your debt elimination goal. Here is a link to an online debt snowball calculator:

https://www.nerdwallet.com/blog/finance/debt-snowball-calculator/

Before you begin aggressively attacking debt, make sure you have an emergency fund! Your emergency fund should be enough to cover at least one month of expenses while paying off consumer debt. If you cannot do this, try to save at least a week's pay in savings.

NEGOTIATING WITH YOUR LENDERS

First list out all of your debts along with the creditor's name. If you are behind, see how much you are behind with your payments. Then make a list of most important debt to least important debt. (Ex. 1. Mortgage or Past due rent, 2. Car loan, 3. Utility bills, 4. Federal loans, 5. Student loans. These are the debts that you should negotiate first. Before calling any of your creditors, try to increase your income or show the creditor that you are taking steps in the right direction for your finances. Then call your creditors and ask for a lower monthly payment, lower interest rate, or ask to make interest only payments until you can get back to a healthy monthly income. Make sure to get any type of negotiation agreement in writing. Ask for a supervisor if you are not making progress with the customer service representative assisting you.

Debt Consolidation: I do not recommend consolidating any of your loans. This is often the result of your debts causing you mental stress. Consolidating your loans may sound like a good idea in that moment, but this will actually hurt you more than help you. Many companies offering debt consolidation will also offer a high interest loan to "help" you pay off your debts faster. Just stay away from this. However, some lenders will offer a lower interest rate. But this is never to help you in the long term. Lower interest rates are subject to change at the discretion of the lender, specifically when it comes to transferring credit card balances. In the event that you are trying to lump several debts together, always run the numbers for the amount of interest you will pay over time. This is how many lenders trick people into consolidating loans. For example, say you have two loans: $10,000 for a personal loan with an interest rate of 12 percent for two years and $20,000 for a car with an interest rate of 10 percent for four years. Your current total monthly payment is $1,100 for both payments. You then apply to consolidate the two loans and the new lender offers a combined monthly payment of $640 with a 9 percent interest rate for six years. It seems more affordable for the short term when you are struggling financially. This will end up costing you an additional two years with an additional $5,688 more in interest payments. Lenders are never here to help you, even with easier, short-term options.

Refinancing: Refinancing might make sense only for those truly struggling to pay their debts. By refinancing a loan, you are accepting a lower interest rate for that particular debt if you have a "good" credit score. However, this also means that a new loan is given, which could potentially cause you to take longer to pay off the loan, especially when there is no plan. Look carefully at the terms of the refinancing agreement. Avoid refinancing for consumer debts. Refinancing credit cards, car loans, and personal loans is essentially ineffective since it is moving one loan balance to another. If possible, only consider huge loans such as student loans or mortgages when refinancing for a better interest rate. However, refinancing is also not a recommendation to getting out of debt quicker because it restarts your loan payment plan.

Debt Settlement: Stay away from any person claiming that they can get rid of any debts on your credit reports. This will negatively impact your credit report, which you want to always keep clean. Never hire someone to help you "fix your credit," most of them are scams because your credit report will fix itself as long as you do not ignore it. Negative remarks will fall off of your report seven to ten years after it is reported. So, if you find that you truly need help with your debt, make sure that you contact a credit counseling agency that has a history of helping individuals settle the debts themselves. The best way to fix your credit is to have an understanding of your report as well as what you legally owe. No decisions to creditors should be made without your consent and understanding of any plans created in writing.

Bankruptcy: This should be the very last resort. Bankruptcy is usually only a temporary fix to long term thinking that got you into debt in the first place. There are two main kinds of bankruptcy: Chapter 7 and Chapter 13. A Chapter 7 is when most of your debt is wiped out usually at the expense of having to give up some form of property. It also does not require you to repay any of the debts you owed because it is usually meant for people with limited incomes. A Chapter 13 bankruptcy requires a debtor to repay some of the debt back under a repayment plan. Chapter 13 allows you to keep some property such as your home or car. If your income is not below a certain amount, a Chapter 13 may be more ideal if you do not qualify for a Chapter 7. Chapter 13 also requires you to pay your debt back within three to five years. Both will negatively impact your credit score and report. This is not recommended, but if all hope seems to be lost, contact a bankruptcy attorney before going through with this option.

Getting out of debt is a mentality. I know for myself, I made temporary sacrifices and got side hustles in order to increase my income and aggressively pay off my student loans. If you have consumer debt, student loans and a mortgage, aim to attack consumer debt first since these usually have higher interest rates and no benefits. Paying off consumer debt should only take up to two years and no more than three if you get serious and follow a plan as well as cut out unnecessary spending while increasing income.

Most people are not willing to take on additional jobs to get out of debt faster, and usually fall subject to one of the above-mentioned options because it feels easier. Easier is what got you into to debt and easier will keep you in debt. There must be a sense of urgency when trying to build your future, especially when time is of the essence. The reality is, the older you are, the less time you have to build for your future. So only you can do what is best for your life, sometimes that means getting uncomfortable for a short period of time and doing what is hard.

STUDENT LOANS

After you have paid off consumer debts, aggressively attack student loans. Why wait 10, 20, or 25 years to pay off student loans in the forgiveness programs that most people will not qualify for anyway?

Not so fun fact: did you know that only 1 percent of the people who applied for the public service loan forgiveness program were accepted? That is right! That means that 99 percent of all applicants were rejected. The only loans accepted under the current loan forgiveness program are Direct Federal Loans. The program also requires 120 consecutive payments to qualify while working full-time in a specific government, teaching, or non-profit position. Private loans and other federal loans will not be forgiven.

If you have any private loans, pay off any of these loans first because these loans usually have higher interest rates than federal loans. After making extra payments toward private student loans, attack federal loans aggressively. Never default on student loans because after a while, the lenders can begin to garnish wages. If you are currently on a deferment or forbearance option, do your very best to at least come up with a plan to make the minimum payment. By not paying anything, your loan will balloon, making the problem worse than before.

Here are some of the options for payment plans for student loans other than the Ten-Year Standard Plan:

1. Graduated Repayment Plan: Payments start off low and then increase every two years up to ten

years.

2. Extended Payment Plan: Payment plan extended up to twenty-five years.

3. Pay as You Earn Plan: Payment is equal to 10 percent of annual income, but it will never be more than what the payment would be under the standard plan.

4. Revised Pay as You Earn Plan: Payment of 10 percent of annual income.

5. Income Based Repayment Plan: Payment of 10 to 15 percent of your annual income.

6. Income-Contingent Repayment Plan: Payment will be 20 percent of disposable income or an agreed fixed payment for twelve years, whichever is less.

7. Income Sensitive Repayment Plan: A fifteen-year plan that causes your payment to increase or decrease depending on your annual income.

To learn more about each plan, visit studentaid.ed.gov.

I HAVE MASSIVE STUDENT LOAN DEBT AND I CANNOT AFFORD THE PAYMENT!

It is okay! Relax. You are not alone. Many people took on student loan debt by lack of understanding, transferring schools, switching majors, using the loans to live beyond their means, or taking longer than four years to graduate. One major reason for high student loan debt is receiving a professional or graduate degree. It is more common than people realize. If you owe $80,000, $90,000, $150,000 or more, there is still a plan to pay them off in five years or less after paying off consumer debt.

Whether you have private or Federal student loans, do not stress. Following the steps below will guide you through.

1. Understand your loans.
2. Review your current repayment plan (student loan plans listed above).
3. Separate private and Federal loans.
4. Understand how your lender accepts extra payments. If need be, contact your lender to make sure you know how extra payments will be applied to your student loans (*is your payment going only to interest?*).
5. Increase your income by at least the minimum payment.

6. Organize student loans from smallest to largest.
7. Rank the interest rates from smallest to largest.
8. If you have a high income, look to refinance any private loans, **only** *if* the refinancing option is for a shorter repayment term with a lower interest rate. Check out if refinancing may be right for you at Credible.com.
9. Create a pay-off plan and put in a specific pay-off date, which will determine when your student loans will be paid off (*most lenders have a tool that allows you to calculate your pay-off date on their website*).
10. Pay off private, high interest loans first.
11. Pay off each Federal loan one by one.
12. If you are sticking to a spending plan, it may make sense to set up an automatic payment from your checking account because this helps reduce the interest rate of the loans usually by 0.25 percent, which allows more money to go to the principal.
13. Pay extra on student loans (*ex. I am going to pay an extra $200 a month toward my student*

loan balance).
14.   Keep living expenses low.

An example of a student loan repayment plan is listed below for your reference. Here, you will see that the private student loan is first because of the higher interest rate and the other federal loans are listed in the order to which they should be paid. This is a combination of the debt snowball and the debt avalanche.

HOW TO PAY OFF STUDENT LOANS

Student Loan Type	Current Price	Interest Rate	Minimum Payment
Private Loan	$5,500	6.8%	$90
Direct Unsubsidized	$3,030	3.61%	$30
Direct Unsubsidized	$3,500	3.61%	$40
Direct Subsidized	$5,500	4.41%	$50
Direct Subsidized	$5,500	4.41%	$50

Using the list above, if you wanted to be debt free by December 2020 with your debt freedom plan beginning in August of 2019, you would need to pay a total of $1,400 a month, which is an additional $1,140 of extra payments toward student loans. This may seem like a lot of extra money per month; however, you have to get intentional especially when paying off debt even if your extra debt payment is not as much as the above number.

Note: Direct subsidized and unsubsidized loans are student loans offered by the federal government. Subsidized loans are based on financial need and interest does not accrue while the borrower is still in college because the interest is paid by the federal government. Only undergraduate students qualify for direct subsidized student loans. Graduate and professional students cannot receive direct subsidized student loans, however, they may receive unsubsidized. So, the interest accrues the moment a student takes out the unsubsidized student loan, which is why the balance is higher than the original loan.

EMPLOYMENT STUDENT LOAN PAYMENT ASSISTANCE

Another option could be finding a job that will offer student loan payment assistance for a portion of your student loans, usually $1,000 to $5,000 a year and max out after a certain number. Some employers offer this benefit to their employees as an incentive in compensation packages. Some employers include: Aetna, Chegg, Fidelity Investments, First Republic, Staples, and

PricewaterhouseCoopers (PwC).

Moreover, in certain fields such nursing or certain government position, employers may assist with student loan assistance as well.

TAX BENEFITS FOR PAYING INTEREST ON YOUR STUDENT LOANS

Finally, if you make less than $70,000 per year as a single filer or $140,000 per year married filing jointly, then you can deduct up to $2,500 a year from your taxable income for the interest paid. However, if your income is between $70,000 to $85,000 as a single filer or $140,000 to $170,000 as married filing jointly, you can deduct a partial amount of the $2,500, but any income above those amounts disqualifies you from receiving this tax credit. Make sure to look on your lender's website to get a copy of how much interest you have paid on your student loans each year by viewing a Form 1098-E, student loan interest statement when tax season comes around.

HOW YOU CAN AVOID STUDENT LOANS

For different stages of life, student loans have either been issued to you, are about to be issued to you, or you are a parent who wants to avoid this trap for your children. No worries! For the latter options, here is what you should do in order to avoid student loans.

Stay away from For Profit colleges, especially those seeking an education in their later years. According to a recent study that was conducted by the Center for Analysis of Postsecondary Education and Employment, the majority of those who enrolled in For Profit colleges did not graduate with their degrees (about twenty-two percent graduate), leading to high student loan debt with lower incomes or no employment at all. This has led to higher rates of defaulting on (failing to pay back loans, which creates delinquency) student loans, especially among African American women.

Attend community college or go to trade school. Only attend private colleges if you have the cash to pay for it, including scholarships. Otherwise, the incentive to attend private education is not greater than the benefit of the debt collected. Trust me, I attended a private university my freshman year of college, which was the reason for majority of my student loan debt.

MY STORY

I did several things in college to avoid adding more student loan debt. First, I transferred universities and went from a private college to an in-state public college, which decreased my tuition by $28,000 per year. Second, I worked three jobs my sophomore through senior years. To name a few: I was a pizza delivery driver, office assistant, daycare assistant teacher, night auditor at a hotel, intern at a couple major companies, temporary employee for FedEx, and a book sales assistant.

My senior year, I was a basketball coach, worked in the economics department as a research assistant, and was an intern at a local law firm. I was specific with my job choice during this year because it provided me with the opportunity to have a flexible schedule. My research assistant position was a job that I could work from home. And my coaching job was an evening and Saturday job. This helped me tremendously as I was earning more than what I needed to pay for my remaining tuition with cash.

Third, I took the max amount of credit hours that I could take for a semester so that I could graduate early as well as took fast paced 4-week free courses offered by my university during the summer of my rising senior year.

Lastly, I moved off campus into an apartment with 1 to 2 roommates where we split expenses which decreased my living expenses by nearly 40 percent by not having to pay for a dorm or a college meal plan. This allowed me to budget my food for groceries to buy only what I needed.

I did all of this in addition to applying for scholarships. My total college scholarship package was $35,000 for three and a half years of school, which was about one-third of the total actual costs of my college education.

One thing I wish I had done in high school was apply for even more scholarships. A good rule of thumb is to expect to win 1 out of 20 scholarships applied for. Winning money for college may seem like a challenge, but it is definitely possible. Two great websites for college scholarships are: scholarships.com and myscholly.com

I know, working this hard may seem like it is not doable, but it is. Furthermore, I guarantee you the joy that I had graduating college in a more cost-efficient way was indescribable. This philosophy enabled me to be able to pay off the student loans that I had accumulated my first two years quickly. Working while in college is vital for success. I missed out on a lot of "fun," however, I have zero regrets as the average student is graduating with $37,000 of student loan debt today.

GRADUATE SCHOOL

Going to graduate school or professional school for free or for the least amount of debt possible can be done by implementing the following action steps:

1. Determine if grad school is even necessary for your career path. Does the cost outweigh the expected income after graduation?
2. Compare the graduate programs of several different schools.
3. Create a LinkedIn account if you do not have one already (all professionals should have one). Research the number of graduates from the program of your interest and look at their job titles.
4. Take a gap year and work to save.

5. Go to a one-year program.
6. Become a TA or graduate assistant to pay for your education.
7. Work during your time in school and cashflow your education.
8. Apply for scholarships.

SAVING FOR COLLEGE

For parents, you should save up money for your children. Do not claim that you can buy $100 shoes for your child or spend $500 on Christmas gifts, but cannot afford to invest in their college education.

Two options to save for college are saving in an investment brokerage account or a 529 college savings plan that enables you to save for future colleges for each of your children. An investment brokerage account at a firm like Fidelity or Vanguard gives you the option to use the money saved for a child for something else if your child does not attend college in the future.

A 529 plan has restrictions only to be used for educational purposes. With a 529 plan, anyone can contribute. Also, the money in a 529 account can be transferred to another child's account if one of the children does not attend college. A 529 account can be used for undergraduate as well as graduate school at any age. Contributions can be made while the recipient is still in school as well. By saving $50 per month for 22 years, that alone would be worth $35,000, and investing $75 per month for 22 years would be worth $52,000. Make the sacrifice to save for your children. Even if you start late, there is still an opportunity to save something for your children.

Depending on the state that you live in, you have different requirements for a 529 plan. You can also save in another state that you might find more preferable. I would do an estimate for the cost of what a college education for your child will be by the time that they graduate high school. A good rule of thumb is to multiply your child's age by $2,000 each year to determine how much to save or invest that year. Then save each month in those accounts. For example, if your child is 7 years old, you should multiple 7 by $2,000 to get $14,000 or $1,167 per month.

However, this may be too much for some, so it is recommended to see a financial planner or advisor so they can help guide you in this situation. There are ways to do this. If you cannot afford a financial planner or advisor, consult a robo-advisor through Betterment, Wealthfront, or Vanguard. Robo-advisors are automated, online investment management services, which means that your investments are handled by a software program rather than a human advisor. This is a much more affordable option often for people just getting started or those who have less complicated investments. However, a good goal is to have enough money to send your child to an in-state, public university. When it comes time to go to college, allow them to live at home with you to save money on housing. Try saving at least $50,000 for each child by the time they graduate.

Visit investor.vanguard.com/529-plan/ to learn more about saving for your child's college. However, do not save for your child's college at the expense of your financial future. Get out of consumer debt first.

A 529 should always be used for the child. Even if your child wins a full scholarship, they can use it for graduate or professional school. In the event that your child does not go to college, it can still be used for them. You can even give this money to your child in order to purchase a home later. However, there will be a penalty for using the money for anything other than education.

PAYING OFF COLLECTIONS

This means that you have not paid bills on time and this affects your credit score negatively even if you do not have actual debt.

Before paying off anything in collections, verify the amount with the collector who purchased your balance owed. Make sure you understand how to pay and whom to pay, but never give them your account information. If your balance is really high, try negotiating the amount to pay and include that your credit report needs to be updated upon receipt of payments. Never do any of this without getting it in writing first. Keep records of payments for yourself.

PAYING OFF YOUR MORTGAGE EARLY

Paying off your mortgage early may seem like it is impossible. However, with the right strategy, it can be made possible. Below is a four-step method that will help you pay off your mortgage early if you desire.

1. Switch to biweekly payments. This allows 13 payments in a year instead of 12.

2. Make extra principal payments. You will need to contact your mortgage lender directly in order to instruct them on "principal only" payments or they will add it to the interest if you do not inform them of how the extra payment should be applied.

3. Refinance to a shorter-term loan if your spending plan allows. If you have a 30-year term, switch to a 15-year fixed term.

4. If you get a raise or tax refund, put the additional money toward the principal payment.

You are only to pay off your mortgage early if you are completely out of consumer debt and have a 4-6 month emergency fund in place.

The next image is the depiction of a payment plan for a conventional 30-year vs. a conventional 15-year fixed loan. The monthly payment is higher for the 15-year fixed loan, but the interest saved over time is worth the higher payment.

BUILDING EQUITY FASTER – A COMPARISON

Mortgage Term	30 years	15 years
Loan Amount	$118,000	$118,000
Months to Pay	360	180
Annual Rate	4.0%	3.0%
Monthly Payment	$563	$815
Total Interest	$84,806	$28,680
Interest Savings	–	$56,126

Your mortgage should be the last debt you plan to pay off early. Know that your house is not an investment; it is an asset and should be seen as a blessing, not a financial curse.

Visit the link below to determine how quickly you can pay off your mortgage:

www.bankrate.com/calculators/mortgages/mortgage-loan-payoff-calculator.aspx

Step 8:

SAVE SIX MONTHS OF EXPENSES

Remember when I said to be your own credit card? Well you should apply that same principle to now creating a fully funded emergency fund. Having a fully funded emergency fund is necessary to pay for major, unforeseen losses. Unforeseen circumstances are categorized as: large house maintenance expenses, wanting to change jobs, losing a job, or becoming ill. It takes a person an average of two to three months to get a new job after losing one. By having a fully funded emergency fund, a job loss becomes an inconvenience instead of a disaster. Remember, you have a buffer and Car Fund to handle anything else in regard to replacing a car or fixing things. Your emergency fund is for emergencies.

Building this fully funded emergency fund is only for those who have no consumer debt. After your 24 to 36 months of paying off all of your consumer debt, you now will pause your debt payment plan. This means that you only have a mortgage or student loans left. By temporarily pausing extra debt payments to build your emergency fund, you are putting yourself in a position to win financially. It may take some time to build a fully funded emergency fund so only make minimum payments on your student loans and/or mortgage while saving.

In addition, if you get a bonus at work or any unexpected income, try saving at least 90 percent of your bonus to fund your emergency fund. If you get a tax return, I highly recommend that you use all of that to fund your emergency fund because this is money that the government took away from your paychecks throughout the year. A tax refund is not extra money. The quicker you can save up your six-month emergency fund, the better. If you feel that you will not need a six-month emergency fund, aim for at least four months. I only recommend having a minimum of four months of expenses saved if you are married or live with a partner. If you are single, I suggest that you aim for six months.

Again, an emergency fund should consist of at least all of your monthly fixed expenses. If it will make you feel comfortable, you can now add in some variable expenses such as groceries or eating out just to give you some wiggle room. However, this is not a requirement and will make your savings process even longer.

STEP 9:

INVEST IN ASSETS AND THE PROPER INSURANCE

When trying to build wealth through investing, the first objective is to eliminate any and all consumer debt. The second objective is to have an adequate emergency fund, so you avoid more debt and avoid the temptation of using your investments for emergencies. Then you will be able to afford to invest. Earning money from your employer and receiving income raises will not mean much if you do not learn how to invest your money.

Many people are afraid to invest, but not afraid to go into debt when debt causes their income to become negative. Investments can only go to zero, however, for those who make smart investments, this would only be temporary.

While you are paying off consumer debt, you should not be investing into retirement accounts such as your 401k and Individual Retirement Arrangements (IRAs) unless you are 45 and older. However, if you are out of consumer debt, you definitely should be investing at minimum in a 401k or 403b account. If your employer does not offer a 401k or other form of retirement savings such as a 403b or government sponsored retirement plan, then you can still invest for retirement in IRAs.

THE RULE OF 25

The Rule of 25 is a tool used to determine how much you will need to save for your retirement. This amount is 25 multiplied by your annual expenses. For example, if your income is $60,000 a year and you spend $40,000 a year, you will need to multiply $40,000 by 25 to get $1,000,000 for your retirement number. This is a great rule to determine if you will be able to retire.

For some, this may not be enough, especially those wanting to retire early, but this could be a great start into creating a plan. You must also consider inflation and pay raises. So, to over-prepare for retirement, a good number to feel more than comfortable may be to use a number that is 30 to 40 times your annual expenses.

Moreover, this rule works best for those without any debt. So, if you plan to retire with debt, calculate that into your retirement plan as well.

YOUR RETIREMENT

A 401k or 403b is a tax-deferred retirement plan where employees can contribute a percentage of their income with their pre-tax dollars. This means that the employee will pay taxes upon withdrawal and not at the time of contribution, unless his or her employee offers a Roth 401k, which is where employees contribute with their after-tax dollars and will not have to pay taxes later. If your employer offers a Roth 401k, take advantage of this. What many fail to realize is that these accounts are investing in the market, but the choices are limited by the plans your company has chosen for you. You are responsible for contributing and finding out which investment options (stocks, mutual funds, bonds) your plan has.

Employees under the age of 50 can contribute up to $19,000 per year in 401k and 403b accounts in 2019, which adjusts to roughly $500 per year due to inflation. Employees over 50 years old can contribute an additional $6,000 per year, which would be $25,000 per year as of 2019.

Go to retirementplans.vanguard.com to calculate how much money you need to invest to live comfortably in retirement. Most companies automatically enroll employees into the plan after a month in a Target Date Retirement Fund, contributing 3-6 percent of his or her income.

THE TARGET DATE FUNDS

Target Date Retirement Funds are investment options based on an employee's specific retirement date (when the employee turns 65). For example, for someone who is 40, his or her target retirement year would be around 2045. Target dates may not be the specific year that employee would actually retire because these funds are in increments of five years.

The Target Date Funds are allocated into a mix of stocks, bonds, and other investments that are passively managed by the investment firm that your employer has chosen. The risk of each Target Date Fund is determined by the year an employee is set to retire. So, the younger the employee, the more the risks, which just means the more stocks the portfolio has.

As you near closer to retirement, your portfolio investments become more conservative. The employee also does not get to choose his or her investments, which means that his or her portfolio may contain some investments that may not perform as well as other options. Solely relying on this higher fee investment option may not lead to the wealth you want especially if you are only contributing 3-6 percent of your income per year. Even with the match, the majority of Americans are not saving nearly enough in these accounts that have unsuccessfully replaced pensions.

The graph below shows the average amount people have saved for retirement by age.

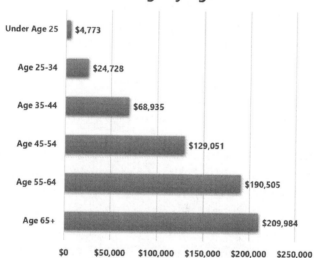

Average Retirement Savings by Age

Under Age 25	$4,773
Age 25-34	$24,728
Age 35-44	$68,935
Age 45-54	$129,051
Age 55-64	$190,505
Age 65+	$209,984

$0 $50,000 $100,000 $150,000 $200,000 $250,000

Source: Vanguard, *How America Saves 2018*

Clearly, with the desired amount to live comfortably in retirement being at least $1.7 million, according to a survey from Charles Schwab, most people are not saving nearly enough for retirement. This is why you should make sure you know how your 401k retirement investments are allocated. There is nothing wrong with having your investments in a Target Date Fund but understand that your employer may have better investment options. In the case that your employer does not offer any other options, you can stick with this choice. A 401k should not be your only investment for building wealth especially if you are younger than 45.

Some people want a simple path to wealth and that may mean maxing out their retirement plans. However, if you want to retire early, you need another strategy.

If you switch jobs, you can rollover your 401k to an IRA or add your old 401k to your new employer 401k. You may also keep your old 401k parked with your old employer although you will no longer be able to contribute to it. However, never take out a 401k loan for yourself or accept the check written to you after leaving a company.

ARE YOU CONTRIBUTING ENOUGH?

Most times, 3-5 percent is not enough to even receive the full company match or employees roll out of the plan due to lack of knowledge of how awesome a company contribution match is for retirement. The earlier you begin to contribute, the better. For example, if your company says that they will match up to a certain percentage, let's say 5 percent, then you should be contributing 5 percent. So, if you make $3,000 per month before taxes, that is a total of $150 per paycheck, and the match will be an additional $150 per paycheck of free money, so you get a 100 percent return in addition to the growth from the compound interest of your investments. If you start at age 22, and only contribute this much for 20 years, you could have $165,442.22 saved by age 42 and $409,328.96 after 30 years using an average rate of return of 8 percent. Since, this is not enough to sustain most people in retirement, because social security is only meant to supplement your income, it is encouraged to contribute more when consumer debts are paid off if you plan on retiring at age 65. If you plan on retiring earlier, you should be investing 20-50 percent of your income in non-retirement investment accounts.

INDIVIDUAL RETIREMENT ARRANGEMENTS

IRAs are Individual Retirement Arrangement (IRA) accounts that offer great tax breaks. You can invest in stocks, bonds, mutual funds and other outside investments such as Real Estate Investment Trusts (REITs). There is much more freedom in choices than with the 401k retirement plans as well as providing lower fees than a 401k charges.

There is a Traditional IRA that is tax-deferred (you take out the taxes later) and the Roth IRA that is funded with after tax dollars (no taxes paid later). Not everyone is eligible for a Roth IRA like with the Traditional IRA. This is why it recommended for those just starting out in their careers to contribute to the Roth IRA. You can contribute to both, but the max amount is $6,000 per year in total or $3,000 per year to each if under 50 years old, but this contribution limit is increased to $7,000 per year if you are 50 years of age and above.

In order to be able to contribute to a Roth IRA, your annual income must be below $122,000 for a single filer or $193,000 filing jointly with a spouse. You can contribute up to a certain percentage if your income is above $122,000 for single filers or $193,000 for those married filing jointly, but the amount phases out up to $137,000 or $203,000 respectively, however, any amount above this makes you ineligible.

For high income earners, there is the opportunity to invest in a Backdoor Roth IRA, which allows you to convert your non-deductible IRA to a Roth even if your income is higher than the income limit. This can be tricky, but doable.

First, you put money into a non-deductible IRA, then convert the account to a Roth IRA, but you will pay your regular taxes on the conversion. Your money then can grow tax-free. Again, this can be tricky to do without the proper guidance, so you should consult with a trusted financial advisor, robo-advisor, or accountant before transferring any funds so that there is no tax liability for improperly converting the funds.

If you are self-employed or are a business owner, you have options as well. Your options can sometimes be better as you can contribute more than the maximums for employer sponsored 401k and 403b retirement plans. Your options are:

- Traditional or Roth IRA
- Simplified Employee Pension Plan (SEP IRA)
- Savings Incentive Match Plan for Employees (SIMPLE IRA)
- Self-Employed 401k plan

- Solo 401k

Combining your 401k and IRA investments for anyone under 50 would be contributing a total of $25,000 per year or $2,083 per month toward retirement accounts. For anyone over 50, the total contribution could be $32,000 per year or $2,667 per month. These are adequate options to help build wealth if you plan to retire at 65 or older, but 401ks can be really expensive due to high administrative costs and expensive investments. Know that there may be better investment alternatives.

EARLY RETIREMENT (Before age 60)

Another option to increase wealth is investing in "early retirement accounts." Early retirement investing is for those who plan to retire earlier than 60. This type of investing is done through non-retirement brokerage accounts at investment banks like Charles Schwab, Vanguard, Morgan Stanley, Fidelity, etc.

There is a reason I separate retirement investing and early retirement investing. For retirement investing, this means you will not be able to access these funds until the age of 59 and a half without a 10 percent penalty. These accounts are not to be used until you absolutely need them. Aim to not use these accounts until you have reached 65-70 years old. At 70 and a half years old, you must begin the "Required Minimum Distribution" phase, which is the minimum amount you must withdraw annually. If you do not begin taking minimum distributions at this age, the IRS can take 50 percent of the amount not taken on time. So, if you are able to, hold out until 70. Unless you have funds in a Roth IRA. In this account, you are never required to withdraw beginning at age 70 and a half. This is another great benefit of a Roth IRA because you can allow the money to continue to grow as long as you want. And here is another benefit of a Roth, you can take out the amount you deposited without the 10 percent penalty under certain conditions prior to age 59 and a half, but you must have had the account open for at least 5 years. However, if you are at least 59 and a half, you may still be subject to a penalty if you have not had the Roth for at least five years.

Early retirement investing is only for people who have no consumer debt and have started saving for retirement. Here's why:
If the average monthly debt payment for

Americans is $2,000 with a mortgage, and $800 a month without a mortgage, it is hard to focus on other goals. Imagine what you could be doing with $800 per month over the course of five years.

In five years, that could be worth a total of $57,494.83 grown with an average return of 8 percent compounded annually.

The first question that must be asked is: have you calculated your retirement number or the amount that you need to have saved up in order to stop working and never need debt again?

Your retirement number does not have to mean working until 65-70 years old. Retirement just means you do not have to work anymore. With the right plan in place, it should take no more than 15 years after debt is paid to build enough to not have to work anymore. After this, you should be able to guarantee that if you lost your job, you would be okay, ensuring that you never have to be confined to a job or debt ever again. That is true freedom.

INVEST IN THE PROPER INSURANCE

Most people are under-insured in most categories. This is another reason for debt.

I will list the main types of insurance that everyone needs at minimum to maintain financial freedom.

Medical Insurance

Many people do not go into retirement thinking about medical costs. It is expensive now more than ever to go for a routine check-up or receive any other basic service from a doctor's office. Still knowing this, most people rather use a credit card to pay for a medical expense than understanding their insurance and neglecting purchasing better medical insurance even after they are no longer working. In the event that you have to go to the emergency room for a couple of days, do you have enough coverage to be able to pay for most of a $15,000 procedure? If the answer is no, it is time to fix this problem. Paying $30 per month for insurance should be an indicator of not being properly insured. You should question why your car insurance is more expensive than your health. You also can reject the insurance offered by your employer if it does not provide you with good options, although it may be more expensive to do so.

Several companies have switched over to high deductible health insurance plans, which offer lower quality insurance. For example, if you have a deductible of $1,500 and make a medical claim for $4,000 after an emergency room visit to your insurance company, under this high deductible healthcare plan, you will be responsible for paying that first $1,500 out-of-pocket since your insurer is only responsible for paying anything above that $1,500 deductible, which for them would be $2,500. However, one of the best creations to offset the flaws of health insurance plans for people who have a high deductible insurance plan is access to a Health Savings Account or HSA, please try to max that out every year. Self-employed and unemployed persons may contribute to an HSA as well.

The current contribution limit for 2019 is $3,500 per person or $7,000 per family including any employer contributions. Moreover, if you are above the age of 55, you can contribute an additional $1,000. So that would be $4,500 per person or $9,000 per married couple. Those who are above the age of 65 may no longer contribute to an HSA.

HSAs are only offered if you have a high deductible insurance plan (your deductible is at least $1,350 for individuals or $2,700 per family), so your employer may not offer this service. Regardless, you should sit down with a Human Resources representative at your company to understand your health insurance and coverage. High deductible plans are created for "healthy" people, so the out-of-pocket cost is high. If you need to obtain supplemental insurance in addition to your HSA, please purchase it. You can purchase supplemental health insurance through Aflac. Relying solely on an HSA with a high deductible plan is not wise because it often leads to medical debt. Make sure you are properly insured.

However, an HSA has great benefits for your future. After you reach a certain amount, you are able to invest that into investments to help it grow even quicker. It is a great asset to use when you are in retirement. You can use your HSA for numerous things not just medical expenses. You can use it for the eye doctor, the dentist, or therapy; and after the age of 65, you can use it for whatever you want without a penalty. This is a secret to wealth that many do not know about. If you change jobs before you retire, you can still use the funds saved in your HSA for medical expenses even if your new employer does not offer one, you just will not be able to continue to make contributions. Make sure you understand the insurance policy of your new employer.

For those without a high deductible health insurance plan, make sure your insurance plan has a low deductible of $500 or below. You should keep at least 20/80 co-insurance and keep co-pays to the doctor between $20-$40. Your policy should cover generic drugs and have a max out-of-pocket clause. Also, use your employer-based Flex Spending Account (FSA) for medical expenses and child care or dependent care for children, if offered.

There are three FSAs. All of these types help increase your spending income for healthcare and decrease gross income for tax benefits. These include: Health FSA, Limited FSA, and Dependent Care FSA. Contribution Limits for each type of FSA:

1. Health FSA=$2,700
2. Limited FSA=$2,700
3. Dependent Care FSA=$5,000 per household

Health FSAs may be used for several types of out-of-pocket health care expenses. Limited FSAs are only for an employee who also contributes to an HSA, so this account can only be used for dental and vision purposes. Dependent Care FSAs may only be used for children up to 13 years old, dependents with disabilities, and elderly care. The money in this account may be used for a child's daycare expenses as well as before and after school care expenses. Each year, you either use the money in this account or you lose it. So, take full advantage.

Unlike an HSA, you cannot rollover your Health FSA dollars from year to year or keep it after you leave your current employer that offers the FSA. However, some employers offer a maximum of $500 to be rolled over from the previous year or a grace period of 2.5 months to spend any unused funds. Both HSAs and FSAs usually offer debit cards to use to allow for a quicker option when needed to spend these funds.

The average healthcare cost in retirement is estimated to be $280,000 per person. Which means if you retire early, you may need well over $300,000 planned in today's dollars. So, a plan must be created to include medical costs in the event that you retire from working.

The average emergency expense ranges from $200-$1,200 per visit. My recommendation for low medical expenses on top of having adequate insurance is good eating habits, exercise, and proper sleep. Also make sure that you actually owe what you are charged because nearly 80 percent of hospital bills contain errors. Sometimes hospitals send you incorrect amounts for your bills. I once had a bill sent to me for $800 that my insurance was supposed to cover, but the hospital continued to send me the bill for months after my emergency room visit. I contacted my insurance company, and they sent me a check for $693. I negotiated with the hospital, and they accepted the check for $693. It might take some time, but it is worth the fight. Always negotiate and verify especially if you have a large medical bill.

Dental and Vision Insurance

The average cost for both dental and vision insurance for one person is $600 per year. Many times, people are unaware of what the insurance actually covers. For many, vision insurance is more like a discount plan because it does not cover what people actually want. However, if you are someone who buys expensive eyewear throughout the year, vision insurance may be for you. If you are someone who only cares about just getting an eye exam or a generic pair of frames, or someone with a family, having an FSA, HSA, or simply self-insuring may be a better option than wasting money on vision insurance because the out of pocket costs may outweigh the benefit of the insurance. As you get into more services such as anti-glare and progressive lenses, many vision plans do not cover more than the lenses and frames because you are given an allowance instead of insurance. This is why vision insurance should be called an allowance or a discount plan instead of insurance as some plans do not even cover lenses or contacts.

The same goes for dental insurance. Many dental insurance plans are 100/80/50 coverage up to $1,000 to $2,000 maximum. Which means that if you are not planning on having a major procedure done such as removing your wisdom teeth, it may not be worth it. Your dental coverage also may be limited to certain dental locations. In addition to not being able to use your insurance everywhere, some dentists charge higher for people with insurance and most dental plans do not cover dentures or braces. So, it is really important to understand what you are paying for.

Disability Insurance

Disability insurance is important to have,

whether your job provides this benefit or not. This is a form of income protection in the event something happens to you that prevents you from working for a period of time. Purchasing additional disability insurance outside of your employer is ideal because the benefit your employer provides may not be adequate enough to sustain a temporary income shortage. Accidents and ailments happen from time to time, so it is always better to plan for it even if it never occurs.

Short term disability helps cover a portion of your income for a short period of time. Long term disability insurance helps cover your income for an extended period of time. This is good to purchase as a supplement because accidents could cause an injury that could cause a permanent disability.

You can purchase supplemental disability insurance through Aflac or by going on Policygenius.com to compare insurers and learn more about which policy is best for you.

Life Insurance

Make sure that you have adequate life insurance and the correct life insurance. Someone who is 35 with small children does not need the same type of life insurance as a 60-year-old with adult children. I recommend getting a twelve-year, Term Life Insurance Policy for those with families that rely on his or her income and to avoid whole life insurance because it can get expensive and not be adequate enough when you need it. Be sure that you receive the correct advice from people in these fields of service that are trusted to give you the right plan for your future. Proper insurance is a way to guarantee that debt will never be needed. GoFundMe is not life insurance or a burial policy. Have life insurance even for your children. Life insurance through your employer is not enough and it ends after you are no longer employed.

For some additional guidance, head over to Policygenius.com to compare term life insurance policies from the top insurers.

Car Insurance

For those with cars, make sure you have more than the minimum coverage. When searching for the optimal car insurance (I recommend Geico or Progressive), you should be making sure that you have adequate coverage for the following at minimum: 1) Bodily injury liability, 2) Property damage liability for another's property, 3) Personal injury protection, 4) Medical payments for you and passengers, 5) Rental car expenses, and 6) Purchase gap insurance, which pays you the difference between your car's value and what you owe on the loan or lease if your car is a total loss, from your insurance company. Your insurance should come with roadside assistance. There is no such thing as "Full Coverage" insurance, however, you can create a dependable package that is comprehensive of both collision and liability insurance.

Renter's Insurance

If you rent, make sure you have renter's insurance to cover your personal belongings in the case of theft, fire, or water damage. You can compare renter's insurance policies on Policygenuis.com.

Homeowner's Insurance

For homeowners, you need to make sure that you have insurance to protect your home. Many with a mortgage believe that the Private Mortgage Insurance (PMI) is to protect the home. However, this will only cover the loan you took out to purchase the home and has nothing to do with protecting your home. Homeowner's insurance protects the property by covering losses and damages to a person's house and assets in the house. It also provides liability coverage against accidents in the house or property. You can find more information regarding homeowner's insurance through Geico or Progressive Insurance.

Umbrella Insurance

You may also need personal umbrella insurance. This policy is for extra liability insurance that goes beyond the limits of the insured's home or auto insurance. This helps protect people from liability claims that may cause you to be responsible for damages or bodily injuries of another. This will help protect your assets. Geico is a great choice for umbrella insurance.

Planning for Long Term Care

For those over 55, purchasing long term care is a must. You do not want your children to be held responsible for all the decisions you should have planned for in the event that your health fails. Children should talk to their parents regarding long term care plans.

Planning Your Life

Also, make sure that you have your Last Will and Testament written along with a Health Care Power of Attorney, Living Will, Digital Asset Protection (for bank account passwords and social media access) and a Financial Power of Attorney. This ensures that your family will not have to pay or lose any money to the court in the case that you pass away suddenly. We must not only plan our lives, but also our deaths. Please plan accordingly by meeting with an Estate Planning attorney to determine how to protect yourself and your assets.

Planning your retirement and being properly insured ensures that debt will be a thing of the past.

Finally, you want to make sure that you invest in the proper insurance, including miscellaneous insurance that is important for a debt free future. That goes for anything that you purchase. Many people go into debt because they do not plan. Not having the proper insurance is one of those ways.

FINAL THOUGHTS

Most people want results without going through the process, when the results they have now are because they avoided doing things the right way in the beginning. Once you realize that building wealth is a marathon, you will trust the process and see that a no debt life is truly living your best life.

By the end of your debt elimination phase, you should have less than ten bills. Know that each bill you have outside necessities is a choice. Operating five to ten bills is ideal for a successful financial portfolio.

Tip from a Millionaire:

Kevin O'Leary, multi-millionaire investor and host of Shark Tank says, "You need to have all your debts paid off by age 45, including your mortgage."

Whether you are 25, 45, or 65, you should plan to be retired having absolutely zero debt. This is true freedom. This is the freedom I want you and anyone who reads this book to have. What are you willing to do to be free?

As I mentioned before, sacrifice and discipline are the only two ways that you can reach financial freedom. Sacrificing is telling yourself no, delaying gratification, and not falling into the trap of lifestyle inflation every time you get a pay raise.

Lifestyle inflation is when you upgrade to a life that you really cannot afford simply because your income has increased. With more income, you should be saving and investing more. You have to understand if you want this success, you have to do what the majority will not do.

Sacrifice is also not living a hard life. Sacrifice is planning your spending every week, working extra hours or getting a part time job to increase your income to accelerate goals, telling your friends and family "it is not in my budget right now," driving a car you can afford instead of an expensive car you do not need, living with as little rent as possible instead of buying a home to impress others, staying at home instead of vacationing every other month, not going into debt for things you did not save up for simply because you said you wanted it, and not buying new outfits because you are in a funk. The truth of the matter is, most people are not sacrificing, they are struggling. The two are not interchangeable.

Struggling requires no change, but sacrifice does. How long do you have to struggle to understand that your way has not and will not work? Struggling to pay bills and then trying to escape the reality of your struggle by overspending cannot be the life you want. It is time to sacrifice so that you can stop existing. It is time to really live. You must get to a place where being good overcomes your insecurities of looking good.

Now, you have gone through the nine steps to help you enter the no debt zone. What once seemed impossible, is now possible. It will be challenging, but with patience, grit, sacrifice, and discipline, you too will be debt free and creating your no debt zone.

For a free debt payment template, visit winwithimpact.com. Also, if you would like an easy to manage, biweekly budgeting template, my Next Level Budgeting template is available on my website. Enter the code "NODEBTZONE" and you will receive 50 percent off the regular price just for purchasing this book.
Happy   financial   freedom!

ABOUT THE AUTHOR

Ashley Brewster was born and raised in Cincinnati, Ohio. At age 17, Ashley was inspired to begin her journey toward financial freedom and inter-generational wealth.

Ashley became focused and financially intentional by studying financial literature, taking courses, and researching proven strategies to build wealth and escape the rat race. After graduating early with her bachelor's degree in political science from The Ohio State University in Columbus, Ohio, Ashley discovered a deep passion for personal finance and wealth building. This passion inspired her to establish Impact Financial Consulting in January 2018 – a consulting firm geared towards motivating financial change and transforming lives.

Ashley has helped several of her clients completely transform their financial lives by eradiating their debt, automating their savings, and innovating their investing through her Neat Spending philosophy.

With the principles shared in this book, Ashley educates her readers on how they can produce the same, lasting financial transformation in their own lives.

Made in the USA
Lexington, KY
13 December 2019